Guide to
Florida Lighthouses

Guide to
Florida Lighthouses

Elinor De Wire

Pineapple Press, Inc.
Sarasota, Florida

For Jon, Jessica and Scott —
the "brightest lights" in my life.

Pineapple Press, Inc.
Sarasota, Florida

Library of Congress Cataloging-in-Publication Data

De Wire, Elinor, 1953-
    Guide to Florida lighthouses / by Elinor De Wire. — 1st ed.
        p.   cm.
    Bibliography: p.
    Includes index.
    ISBN 0-910923-74-4 : $14.95
    1. Lighthouses—Florida—Guide-books.   2. Florida—Description and
travel—1981- —Guide-books.   I. Title.
VK1024.F6D4 1987   87-16835
387.1′55′09759—dc19   CIP

First Edition
        10 9 8 7 6 5

Printed in Hong Kong
Typography by Lubin Typesetting and Literary Services
Design by Frank Cochrane Associates, Sarasota, Florida

Acknowledgments

Special thanks go to Coast Guard Public Affairs Offices, Seventh Coast Guard District, Miami, and Eighth Coast Guard District, New Orleans, for their generosity in making available historical files and photographs of Florida lighthouses. Thanks also go to Joan Morris at the Florida State Archives, Dixie Lee Nims of the Florida Division of Tourism, and the staff of the National Archives in Washington, D.C.

Behind the scenes help and encouragement came from Wayne Wheeler, president of the U.S. Lighthouse Society; Ken Black, director of "America's Lighthouse Museum" at Rockland, Maine; Bill Gill of Mystic Seaport Museum; and my good friends Ray Empey and Hazel Perinchief.

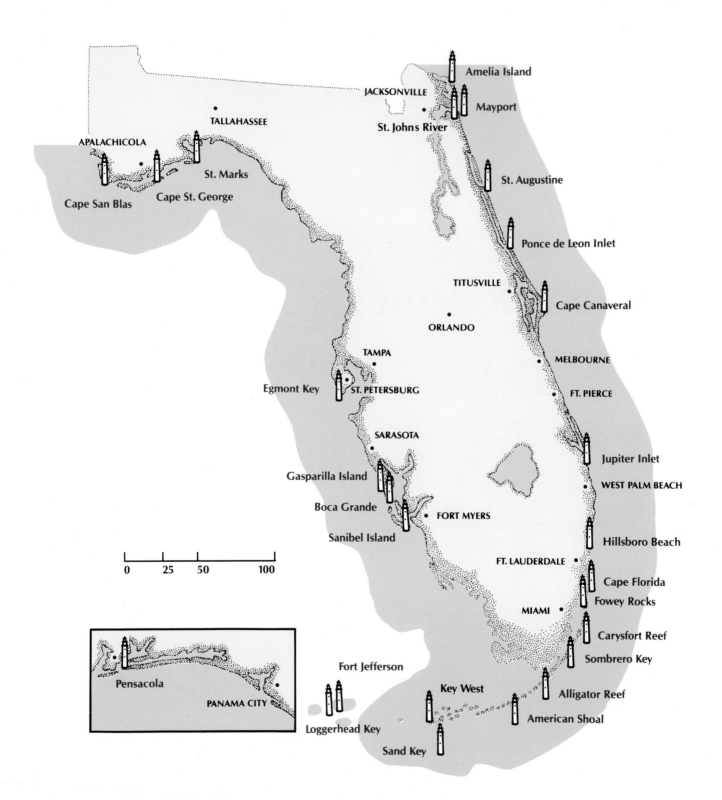

Amelia Island

JACKSONVILLE

Mayport

St. Johns River

TALLAHASSEE

APALACHICOLA

St. Marks

St. Augustine

Cape San Blas   Cape St. George

Ponce de Leon Inlet

TITUSVILLE

Cape Canaveral

ORLANDO

TAMPA

MELBOURNE

Egmont Key   ST. PETERSBURG

FT. PIERCE

SARASOTA

Jupiter Inlet

Gasparilla Island

WEST PALM BEACH

Boca Grande

Sanibel Island   FORT MYERS

Hillsboro Beach

FT. LAUDERDALE

0   25   50   100

Cape Florida

Fowey Rocks

MIAMI

Carysfort Reef

Sombrero Key

Fort Jefferson

Pensacola

PANAMA CITY

Key West

Alligator Reef

American Shoal

Loggerhead Key

Sand Key

Contents

Introduction

The first lighthouse was probably a bonfire set on some coastal hillside to guide home a weary voyager. It lacked the familiar conical shape and sweeping beam associated with today's lighthouses, but it served the same purpose. Later, its signal fire was hoisted onto a pole or hung in an iron basket from a wooden tripod.

Structures resembling today's lighthouses began to appear in ancient times. A 450-foot tower known as the Pharos of Alexandria was the first recorded lighthouse. It was built about 300 B.C. at the estuary of the Nile River, Egypt, and doubled as a temple. This great tower survived 1,400 years before being toppled by an earthquake and was considered to be one of the Seven Wonders of the Ancient World.

By the time the Pilgrims arrived in America, lighthouses were in use throughout Europe, but it was not until 1716 that America's first lighthouse was illuminated. Constructed of stone, it stood on Little Brewster Island in Boston Harbor and was maintained by dues levied on passing vessels. Its beam was produced by candles. A cannon, fired once every half hour in periods of low visibility, served as the colonies' first fog signal.

The benevolent beam of the Boston Lighthouse spawned interest in building other beacons in the colonies. By the time the federal government took over navigational aids in 1789 and established the Lighthouse Service, fifteen lighthouses were active or under construction in the United States. Oil lamps were now illuminating their lanterns,

The world's first recorded lighthouse, the Pharos of Alexandria, stood at the Nile Estuary, Egypt. A 19th century engraver made this representation based on written accounts of the tower.
Photograph courtesy of the Library of Congress.

with whale oil the most popular fuel, but pharology — the science of lighthouse construction and illumination — was moving ahead at a fast pace.

The successful Eddystone Lighthouse in the English Channel had opened up a new avenue for lighthouse engineers faced with exposed, sea-swept construction sites. As the first American pioneers were settling Florida in the early 1800s, another great wave-swept lighthouse was being built on a tortuous rock in the North Sea off the coast of Scotland. It was called Bell Rock, in honor of a legendary bell that once warned mariners of its dangers. Its massive lighthouse and unique lighting apparatus would influence the design of lighthouses for the next century.

In France, a physicist named Augustin Fres-

nel was experimenting with prisms and light. His extraordinary Fresnel lenses were introduced to lighthouses in Europe in 1823 and revolutionized optics. Using prisms' unique reflecting and refracting capabilities, Fresnel arranged them around a light source in such a way as to gather light into a single beam and magnify it many times its original power. Fresnel lenses were differentiated by orders or intensities. A first-order lens produced the most powerful beam and was used for seacoast lights. A sixth-order lens, the weakest, was suitable for harbor beacons of low range.

In 1821, the territory of Florida was annexed to the United States, and, except for an old Spanish watchtower at St. Augustine, no navigational aids stood along Florida's treach-

Boston Lighthouse, America's first sentinel, was built in 1716 on Little Brewster Island. Photograph courtesy of the US Coast Guard.

erous, reef-laden shore. The acquisition of the Louisiana Territory had opened many new ports on the Gulf of Mexico, and commerce increased heavily along the Florida Straits. Shipwreck and piracy increased correspondingly, and both civilian and military seamen pressured the government to mark the Florida Coast and oust its infamous pirates.

St. Augustine's watchtower was hastily examined for possible conversion to a lighthouse, but the government decided it was structurally unsound and built a new tower instead. Though only a harbor light, the 73-foot St. Augustine Lighthouse was Florida's first sentinel and a harbinger of greater towers yet to mark this swiftly growing territory.

In 1822, Secretary of the Navy Smith Thompson recommended a naval depot be set up at Key West to deal with wrecked cargo and provide a support base for United States vessels. Captain David Porter was sent to establish the base and suppress piracy. Congress aided his effort by authorizing the construction of lighthouses at Key West, Dry Tortugas, Key Biscayne, and a lightship at Carysfort Reef. In addition, a lighthouse was built at Pensacola to serve its proposed naval yard.

Carysfort Reef had been given a lightship because of the expense of building a tower on its submerged surface, but at Sand Key, nine miles off Key West, the hard coral reef was covered with a generous layer of sand. A masonry lighthouse was deemed suitable for the tiny key, and a stone tower surrounded by a seawall went into service in 1827. Only a year after Florida was given statehood, its engineers learned an expensive lesson. In 1846, hurricane wind and waves tore away the seawall, toppled the lighthouse, and killed its keeper and her five children.

Masonry towers were obviously not suitable for the unstable, wave-swept Florida Reef. United States lighthouse engineers again looked to Great Britain for the answer. A revolutionary design known as the screw-pile lighthouse had been developed in 1836 by Englishman Alexander Mitchell. It consisted of a lantern perched atop iron piles that were screwed into the soft seabed and, from a distance, resembled a giant spider afloat on the sea. This method of anchoring was ideally suited for the unstable foundations of the southeastern United States, and the open framework of pile towers offered little resistance to hurricane winds and waves.

The development of the screw-pile lighthouse ushered in a new era of lighthouse construction in Florida. In 1852, an iron-pile tower was lit on Carysfort Reef to replace its storm-worn lightship. A year later, Sand Key was illuminated with a pile lighthouse that was anchored to the hard coral beneath its fickle sands. By 1900, more than a dozen pile lighthouses guarded the Florida shore. The genius behind their design and construction was a man who gained fame by defeating the army of General Robert E. Lee at the Battle of Gettysburg. General George Gordon Meade is best remembered for his command of the Army of the Potomac during the Civil War, but his talent as a marine engineer is still in

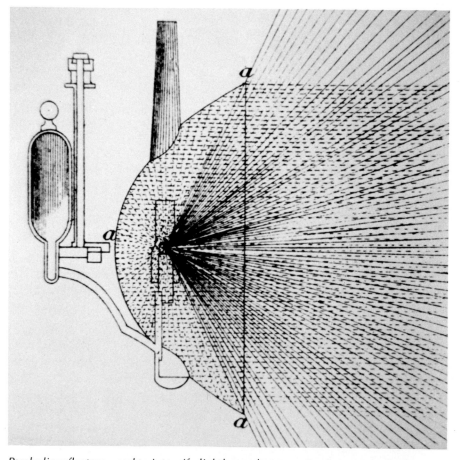

Parabolic reflectors, used to intensify lighthouse beams, came into use in the late 1700s and were later combined with lenses to produce a brilliant beam. Photograph courtesy of the National Archives.

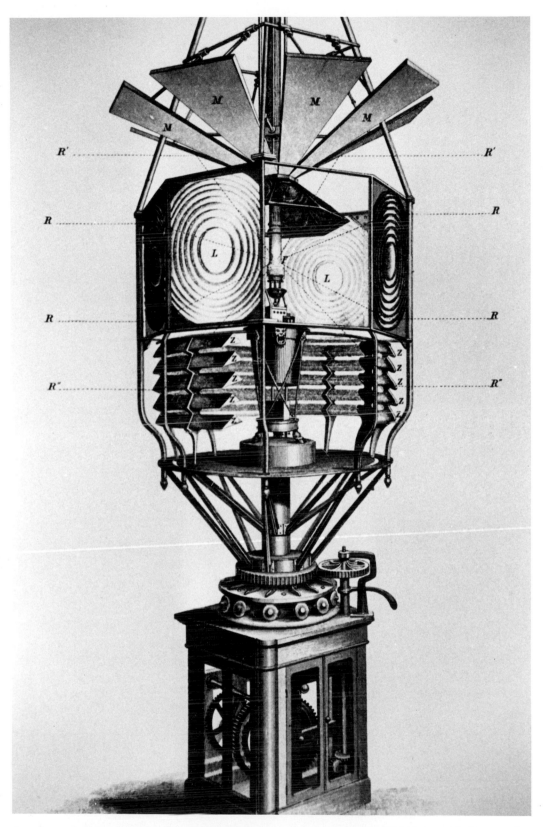

Frenchman Augustin Fresnel invented a revolutionary lenticular optic in 1823 that greatly increased the candlepower of lighthouses. His original lens, pictured here, combined prisms, mirrors, and magnifying bull's-eyes to gather light into a concentrated beam. Photograph courtesy of the National Archives.

The author gets a lightkeeper's view of the world from inside a huge Fresnel lens.
Photograph by Jonathan De Wire.

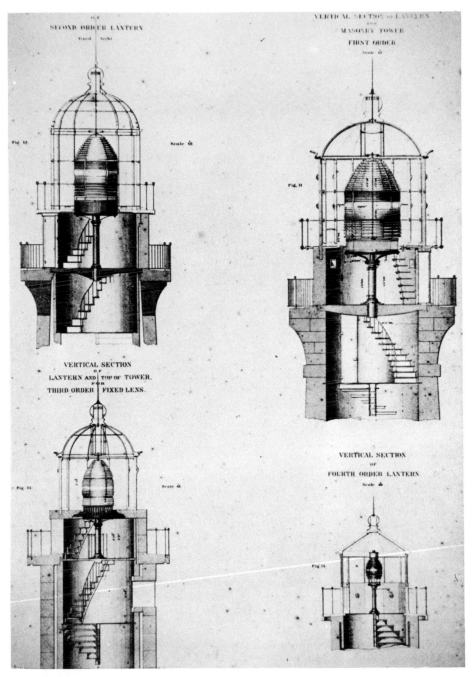

Fresnel's lenses were classified by size and brilliancy. The four largest lenses are pictured here set on their lantern pedestals. Photograph courtesy of the National Archives.

evidence all along the Florida Reef.

After the turn of the century, administration of lighthouses and other navigational aids underwent some changes. A Bureau of Lighthouses replaced the old Lighthouse Board in 1910, and the nation's number of lighthouse districts increased. Many new aids were added, particularly in harbors and rivers. In the interest of economy, the Bureau of Lighthouses was abolished in 1939, and jurisdiction over navigational aids was given to the Coast Guard where it remains today.

Lightkeepers were given the choice between finishing their careers as civilians or

Life aboard a lightship, such as guarded Carysfort Reef prior to 1852, was monotonous. Here lightship crewmen clean the lighting apparatus in preparation for the coming night. Lightship duty was considered among the worst in the Lighthouse Service. Photograph courtesy of the Library of Congress.

joining the Coast Guard with no loss in pay. Most Florida keepers opted for Coast Guard careers, but the era of the lighthouse keeper was drawing to a close. Advances in technology rendered many old sentinels obsolete, and in the 1960s, a program called LAMP (Lighthouse Automation and Modernization Project) eliminated the need for lightkeepers.

Many of Florida's old lightkeepers' homes were boarded up or torn down. Instead of keepers' footsteps echoing up the spiral stairs, light towers hummed and clicked with the machinery of automation. Electric timers and photosensitive cells triggered the lights, and back-up generators kicked on in the event of power failures. Padlocks sealed lighthouse doors, and the historic old beacons were left with only spiders and seabirds for company.

The move to automation was a practical and economic one for the Coast Guard, but it closed a unique and colorful chapter in American history. Without the tender care and devotion of their keepers, lighthouses deteriorated and were vandalized. Their once romantic glow diminished to a feeble glimmer. Saddest of all were the beacons that had been extinguished. Like old soldiers still standing watch, they guarded the shore with dark lanterns.

Public outcry over the neglect of these landmarks spurred the government to seek means of preserving the nation's old sentinels. In Florida, many lighthouses were incorporated into parks, wildlife refuges, and recreational areas. Others were given to their neighboring towns for restoration as museums, or cared for in a cooperative effort between the Coast Guard and local organizations. As a lasting assurance that these Sunshine State relics will not be lost, nearly all have been placed on the National Register of Historic Places.

Some thirty Florida lighthouses today guide shipping south from the St. Marys River to the tip of the keys, then north to Pensacola Bay. They comprise some of Florida's oldest and most historic structures and represent many diverse styles of architecture and daymark designs. Their keepers were among Florida's earliest pioneers — men, women, and children who fought heat, insects, Indians, and sickness to keep the lights burning along Florida's lonely shores. They leave us a wealth of lore and romance that indelibly marks the pages of Florida history.

George Gordon Meade, builder of Florida's giant wave-swept Reef Lights. Photograph courtesy of New York Picture Library.

An artist's conception of life in a lighthouse in the 1880s includes a round living space and leisure activities such as sewing. From St. Nicholas Magazine in the collection of the Library of Congress.
Photograph courtesy of the Library of Congress.

Amelia Island Lighthouse. Photograph courtesy of Florida Division of Tourism.

1

Amelia Island Lighthouse

The St. Marys River forms a natural border between Georgia and Florida and serves as a major artery into the interior of the South. In 1820, a 58-foot brick lighthouse was built on Cumberland Island, Georgia, to mark the river's entrance. Florida was annexed as a territory the following year, and the Lighthouse Service decided the tower could better serve maritime interests on the south bank of the river. Cumberland Lighthouse was dismantled and moved to Amelia Island in 1839.

Other than the installation of a modern lighting system, and a few minor structural repairs, this stalwart sentinel remains little changed from its original design. A touch of Antebellum architecture can be seen in the beautiful granite staircase spiraling up to its rustic iron lantern. Amelia Island Lighthouse's stairs were hand-hewn in New England and transported south by ship. The tower's costly, third-order lens was manufactured in Paris and illuminated with oil lamps.

Amelia Island was named for the daughter of King George II of England and was not only a popular hangout for pirates and smugglers in its early days, but also a thriving reception center during the slave-trading era. In 1818, more than one thousand slaves were brought into this port and smuggled up the St. Marys River via a chain of slave outposts. The men who processed slaves to the interior were called "Moccasin Boys" and knew their territories well.

A 60-ton schooner could hold one hundred fifty standing slaves. Their naked bodies rubbed together until sores opened, and many died from exposure and infection. In order to transport this illegal cargo into port and upriver, the "Moccasin Boys" circulated false rumors of Indian attacks that drove away squatters. The slaves were then moved inland before residents returned.

With United States acquisition of Florida in 1821, and the establishment of Amelia Island Lighthouse two decades later, illegal slave trafficking diminished. The port's importance and the burden of its lightkeeper were increased in the 1850s when Florida's first cross-state railroad was laid from Cedar Key to Amelia Island. Cargoes of lumber, phosphate, and military stores began to arrive and depart, and still later, a great shrimping industry developed.

Amelia Island's stately sentinel remains active today, not only serving the pleasure craft on the Intracoastal Waterway, but the many great tankers of the Atlantic as well. Its automatic beacon operates electrically with a 1,000-watt lightbulb magnified by the century-old prismatic lens. Its 2.5-second white flash is visible nineteen to twenty-three miles at sea. A red sector alerts mariners to the dangerous shoals in Nassau Sound.

The Amelia Island Lighthouse is accessible for viewing on Lighthouse Circle in Fernandina Beach. A replica of the old lighthouse is located on the beach itself and is available as a rental cottage.

Additional Information:

Amelia Island/Fernandina Beach Chamber
of Commerce
Box 472
Fernandina Beach, FL 32034
(904) 261-3248

2  *Florida Lighthouses*

St. Johns River Lighthouses

Two sentinels guard the entrance to Jacksonville's St. Johns River. In a contrast of old and new, these lighthouses stand within a mile of each other on Mayport Naval Station guarding both past and present. One is a gently sloping cylinder of brick capped by a nostalgic iron lantern and gallery. The other is an angular concrete monolith thrusting its warnings into the night with clockwork regularity. Like father and son, they have watched over the river since 1858.

The old St. Johns River Lighthouse is an 80-foot, conical, masonry structure reminiscent of the heyday of lightkeeping. Its early keepers operated an intricate illuminating apparatus powered by huge weights suspended in the tall tower. Working on a principle similar to a cuckoo clock, the weights turned the

lighthouse's French lens and transformed the feeble light of its oil lamps into a blinding beam. An incandescent oil vapor lamp replaced the old system about the turn of the century. Electrification further simplified it in the 1920s, but its lantern is dark today.

The modern St. Johns River Lighthouse succeeded the old beacon in 1954. Often referred to as Mayport Lighthouse, this 64-foot square tower sits on a man-made hill overlooking the estuary and mounts an aeromarine beacon with a white group-flashing sequence visible twenty nautical miles. Attendant personnel operate its radiobeacon — the silent signal that has upstaged so many old lighthouses.

The elder St. Johns River Lighthouse was admitted to the National Register of Historic

Mayport Lighthouse. Photograph by Elinor De Wire.

Old St. Johns River Lighthouse at Mayport. Photograph taken 1900. Photograph courtesy of the Florida State Archives.

Places in 1982, assuring its future preservation. It is a popular landmark with Mayport residents and ferry passengers. Both lighthouses are accessible for viewing on weekends during Mayport Naval Station's open house hours.

Additional Information:

Public Affairs Officer
Mayport Naval Station
Mayport, FL 32228

3  *Florida Lighthouses*

St. Augustine Lighthouse

When Ponce de Leon first sighted the coast of Florida in 1513, there were no navigational aids to guide his ship to a safe anchorage. Using only the stars, rudimentary navigational instruments and his sailor's sense, he put down anchor in St. Augustine, but it was not long before his Spanish followers erected a seamark. Though only a watchtower, it may have held a lamp in its crown. That addition would have made it Florida's first lighthouse, but no evidence has ever surfaced to prove it was.

Following acquisition of Florida in 1821, the U.S. government decided to build lighthouses at several important Florida ports. One of the sites chosen was St. Augustine, the nation's oldest city and earliest port, and the busiest harbor in Florida. Remnants of the three-story stone watchtower were examined and deemed unsound for a lighthouse, but a temporary beacon was placed on it while the new tower was being built.

The new lighthouse was the first official lighthouse in Florida. Completed in 1824, its fourth-order lens was illuminated with oil lamps intensified by bowl-shaped reflectors. It served until the Civil War when Confederates destroyed its lighting apparatus. It was not relit until 1867.

Erosion threatened the St. Augustine Lighthouse by 1870, and with the ocean only 48 feet away, plans were made to relocate it on five acres of land a mile and a half from the old site. Even as the new tower was raised on Anastasia Island, the sea continued to threaten the old tower and came to within 35 feet

St. Augustine Lighthouse. Photograph by Elinor De Wire.

of its base. A jetty of coquina, a white lime-stone composed of broken shells and coral, was quickly constructed to hold back the sea. The second tower was illuminated in October 1874. As if for spite, the sea toppled the old tower in 1880.

St. Augustine Lighthouse is still active to-day, though its keeper has been replaced by automatic machinery. The 161-foot tower retains its beautiful Fresnel lens, emitting a white flash every thirty seconds, and six flights of spiral stairs ascend to the lantern. The lighthouse is painted with Florida's most unique daymark — black and white spiral bands — and is now listed on the National Register of Historic Places. The keeper's residence burned some years ago, but was restored and opened as a museum in 1988 by the Junior Service League of St. Augustine.

The museum contains period furnishings from the lighthouse's early years and interprets its history as both a navigational aid and a St. Augustine landmark. The lighthouse is accessible for viewing on A1A at Anastasia Island just south of St. Augustine and is surrounded by a picnic area and public beach.

Additional Information:

The Junior Service League of
  St. Augustine, Inc.
P.O. Box 244
St. Augustine, FL 32084

4  *Florida Lighthouses*

Ponce de Leon Inlet Lighthouse

Ponce de Leon Inlet was called Mosquito Inlet in 1834 when the first attempt was made to build a lighthouse there. Despite heat, insects and marauding Seminoles, a tower was completed on the New Smyrna side of the inlet, but no light fixture arrived for its lantern. Within a year, storms had undermined its base, and it collapsed.

Fifty years passed before another lighthouse was built, this time on the north side of Mosquito Inlet on a ten-acre plot of the peninsula enclosing the Halifax River and Mosquito Lagoon. The brick for the 175-foot lighthouse, the second tallest on the East Coast, was shipped from Baltimore. Landing materials at the inlet was extremely dangerous, and, during supervision of one of these landings, lighthouse engineer Orville C. Babcock

drowned. The construction of Mosquito Inlet Lighthouse took seven lives in all, casting a dark shadow over its otherwise jubilant lighting on November 1, 1887.

Oil for the remote lighthouse was lightered to the peninsula in small boats, then carried by hand up 203 steps to the lantern. Kerosene later replaced mineral oil in the lamps, and the tower's expensive French lens produced a flashing white light visible twenty nautical miles at sea. Drapes were drawn around it during the day to prevent the sun from cracking its delicate prisms or starting fires. The station was converted to electricity in the 1920s, and the name Mosquito Inlet was changed to Ponce de Leon Inlet.

During Prohibition, rum-runners enroute to the Bahamas often pulled into Ponce de Leon

Inlet at night to avoid trouble on the reefs. Other more legal cargoes sometimes reached Ponce de Leon Inlet's shores as flotsam. Old timers recall one wreck that spewed coconuts over the beaches from Ormond to Ponce Inlet.

In 1970, the historic sentinel was declared surplus since the beacon atop the New Smyrna Coast Guard Station was adequate to aid mariners and much less expensive to maintain than the lighthouse. For two years, the tower stood dark and neglected and at the mercy of vandals. The town of Ponce Inlet repeatedly asked to have the lighthouse. In 1972, the government deeded the tower to the town and efforts were begun to restore it as a museum.

The three keepers' cottages now house nautical and marine displays, lighthouse tools and documents, and the century-old Fresnel lens. In addition, the First Assistant Keeper's house has been furnished in the period of the 1890s when keepers and their families first lived at the station. The lighthouse has a large observation gallery beneath the light room that draws thousands of visitors yearly.

In 1983, it was discovered that construction of a condominium at New Smyrna Beach would eventually obscure the modern beacon atop the Coast Guard Station. The government decided to reactivate Ponce de Leon Inlet Lighthouse. In a ceremony on December 15, 1983, Coast Guard officials and members of the Ponce de Leon Inlet Lighthouse Preservation Association relit the historic old lighthouse and placed it back on the Coast Guard's Light List.

Ponce de Leon Inlet Lighthouse. Photograph by Elinor De Wire.

Ponce de Leon Inlet Lighthouse. Photograph courtesy of Florida Division of Tourism.

A marine aero-beacon replaced the antique Fresnel lens, which remains on display in the museum, and the operative light room was closed off to visitors. Nevertheless, the view from the 160-foot observation deck is worth the strenuous climb up 203 steps. Visitors may note the handholds built into the lantern frame to allow keepers to clean the exterior glass. An occasional chip on the glass panes serves as a reminder of another lighthouse peril — birds colliding with the lantern when confused by its beam.

Additional Information:

Ponce de Leon Inlet Lighthouse Museum
4931 South Peninsula Drive
Ponce Inlet, FL 32019
(904) 761-1821 or (904) 767-3425

Retired Fresnel lens of Ponce de Leon Inlet Lighthouse, now a museum piece.
Photograph by Jonathan De Wire.

5  *Florida Lighthouses*

Cape Canaveral Lighthouse

The black and white banded sentinel of Cape Canaveral seems right at home amid the futuristic landscape of America's space center. Visitors often mistake it for a rocket ready for take-off and are surprised to learn it was one of the first man-made structures to grace the cape. Like its rocket companions of the Mercury missions, Cape Canaveral Lighthouse is capable of movement. The lighthouse, however, only moves when erosion threatens. Its many iron plates and parts can be taken apart, moved, and reassembled like a giant jigsaw puzzle.

The prominent headland it guards was named Cabo del Canaveral by the Spaniards. A strand of dangerous shoals extends out from the cape to imperil shipping headed south with the Labrador Current. In 1848, the government built a 65-foot wooden light tower at Cape Canaveral and installed a feeble beacon in its lantern.

From the very beginning of its career, mariners complained that Cape Canaveral Lighthouse was too dim. It had been built by a local contractor who knew little about navigational needs, but since the Lighthouse Service was embroiled in investigations of scandal and mismanagement, nothing was done about the inadequate light until a decade later.

Just prior to the Civil War, work was begun on a new tower. In addition to increasing the station's range, it was to be the solution to a persistent problem at Cape Canaveral — erosion. The cape was continually being eroded by the sea, and engineers were faced with a

Cape Canaveral Lighthouse. Photograph by Elinor De Wire.

dilemma. If a lighthouse were built near the sea, its beacon would have a substantial range, but the encroaching water could easily undermine it. Built far inland, the tower would be safe from erosion, but inadequate to cover the cape's sprawling shoals.

Final work on the lighthouse was delayed until after the war. It was illuminated in 1868 with the distinction of being one of the nation's earliest relocatable lighthouses. The 139-foot sentinel consisted of detachable cast-iron plates braced together and bolted securely to a concrete base. The interior was lined with bricks for added stability in Florida's hurricane winds. An iron spiral stairway and lantern cap finished the design. The entire structure was capable of being dismantled, moved and reassembled for a fraction of the time and expense of building a new tower.

Just such an occasion arose in 1893. As anticipated, the shoreline eroded toward the lighthouse and threatened to undermine it. The tower was quickly dismantled and reassembled on a safer site where it remains today. Should the sea again threaten, Cape Canaveral Lighthouse can easily be moved.

When lightkeepers first took up residence at the cape, wildlife was more abundant than it is today. Smudge pots and palmetto switches helped ward off the clouds of mosquitoes that were drawn to the beacon. Rattlesnakes clambered onto the cool, exterior stairway of the tower for relief from the heat. It is rumored that one keeper even used the oil of the snakes to lubricate the lens mechanism.

Captain Mills Burnham, one of Cape Canaveral Light's early keepers, planted an orange grove near the tower and also harvested green turtles for the soup tureens of Charleston, South Carolina. Burnham was a well-known and respected resident of the cape for many years. His tenure as lightkeeper was followed by a three-year term in the Florida legislature.

During World War II, the tanker *Pan Massachusetts* was torpedoed off the cape by a German submarine. Her cargo of 100,000 barrels of oil, gasoline and kerosene exploded into flames and set the ocean on fire for a square mile around the lighthouse. It was discovered that enemy submarines lurked in a deepwater area off the cape and could easily spot passing tankers in the beam of the lighthouse. The government extinguished Cape Canaveral Light until the war's end. Still, the British ship *Paz* was hit within a few months of the *Pan Massachusetts* disaster. The *Paz*'s cargo delighted cape residents when it washed ashore — 2,000 cases of fine Scotch whisky.

Cape Canaveral Lighthouse remains active today and is a highlight of the Kennedy Space Center Spaceport bus tour. From a distance, it does resemble a rocket poised for launch, but closer inspection will reveal its "cockpit" contains a beautiful prismatic lens rather than astronauts. Dozens of burned-up launch pads from early Mercury flights surround it. Proudly, this patriarch of the cape has participated in a unique segment of American history. Its beacon has signaled to ships of both sea and air, and its career has transcended many eras in transportation.

Additional Information:

Spaceport USASM
Visitors Center TWS
Kennedy Space Center, FL 32899
(305) 452-2121

6  *Florida Lighthouses*

Jupiter Inlet Lighthouse

Offshore of Jupiter Island, where the Loxahatchee River flows into the Atlantic Ocean, is a reef dreaded by mariners. As ships approach Florida from the east, they must cross the Gulf Stream before heading north. Jupiter's reef is a treacherous obstacle. Congress recognized this in 1853 and authorized the construction of Jupiter Inlet Lighthouse on the north side of the inlet. With a range of eighteen miles, it served as both a landfall light and a coastal beacon for traffic on the Indian and Loxahatchee rivers.

The 105-foot brick tower was designed by George Gordon Meade. He built many of Florida's lighthouses, including the revolutionary screw-pile lights of the Florida Reef, but went on to become immortalized as the man who defeated General Robert E. Lee at

the Battle of Gettysburg. Jupiter Lighthouse was designed to be functional and sturdy, but Meade gave it numerous flourishes, such as portholes over the lantern gallery and a beautiful iron latticework frame for the lantern windows.

Since the inlet was closed in the 1850s, building materials were transported through the Indian River Inlet, then lightered on scows down a tortuous, thirty-five-mile stretch of the river where depth averaged only twenty feet. Fifty such trips escalated the cost of construction to nearly double the original appropriation. As with other Florida lighthouse projects, heat, insects and Indians caused delays. The tower was finally lit in July of 1860 on a forty-foot oyster shell mound left by prehistoric Indians.

Jupiter Inlet Lighthouse. Photograph courtesy of Florida Division of Tourism.

Inside the operative lens at Jupiter Inlet Lighthouse. Photograph by Jonathon De Wire.

The flame had barely been touched to the lamps of Jupiter Inlet Lighthouse when the Civil War extinguished them. Confederate sympathizers removed the illuminating apparatus and buried it in Jupiter Creek. At the end of the war, a government agent and the newly appointed keeper, Captain James Amour, recovered the lighting mechanism and reinstated the lighthouse in June 1866. Captain Amour's forty-year career at Jupiter Lighthouse was one of the longest in Lighthouse service records. His daughter, Katherine Amour, was the first white child born in Jupiter.

By 1900, Jupiter had begun to grow. A life-saving station had been set up at the inlet in 1885 to deal with shipwrecks. The influx of pioneers had necessitated the building of a schoolhouse. Many of Jupiter's early school teachers married lightkeepers, perhaps because they were among the few bachelors living in the area. A number of lighthouse families remained after their tours were completed. The surnames of Jupiter's lightkeepers can be found on the town census even today.

In its early years, Jupiter was also the hub of mid-coast Florida transportation. The route of the Indian River Steamer ended here, and Florida's famed "Celestial Railroad" began at Jupiter and ran through Mars, Venus, and

Juno. In addition, a telegraph station was built on the grounds of the lighthouse in 1911.

During a severe hurricane in 1928, the lighthouse's newly installed electrical system failed, and its cantankerous emergency generator would not start. Fearing for the ships in need of Jupiter Light, Franklin Seabrook, the sixteen-year-old son of the ill head keeper, ascended the tower and began turning the light by hand. At the height of the storm, a portion of the lantern's expensive Fresnel lens was shattered, but young Franklin kept it turning until the generator was repaired two days later.

Shards of the broken lens were salvaged and shipped to Charleston, South Carolina, for repair. Refitting hundreds of prism pieces was no easy task, but the huge Jupiter lens could not be replaced, and its service was indispensable. The shattered magnifying bulls-eye was tediously cemented back together and bound with an iron criss-cross framework. It was returned to the lighthouse and continues in service today.

In June 1973, the Jupiter Lighthouse Museum was set up by the Loxahatchee Historical Society in the fuel-oil storage building at the base of the tower. The lighthouse and grounds were groomed for visitors, and the station was placed on the National Register of Historic Places. Historical memorabilia from the station's century-long career is showcased in the museum. Visitors will find the station's fifty-year-old banyan tree below the lighthouse. A small cemetery near the station entrance contains the bodies of several lightkeepers' children — a sober reminder of the hardships suffered by Florida's early pioneers.

Visitors are welcomed only on Sundays from noon to 2:30 P.M. A guide from the Loxahatchie Historical Society is available to answer questions and trace the history of Jupiter and its lighthouse. Climbing the tower is prohibited, since the lighthouse is still on active duty. However, visitors may peer up the spiral stairway for a giddy view of the lantern.

Additional Information:

Loxahatchee Historical Society, Inc.
P.O. Box 1506
Jupiter, FL 33458

JUPITER LIGHTHOUSE

... ...

Designed by George G. Meade, later Federal commander at Gettysburg. First lighted July 10, 1860. Dark during the War Between the States and its mechanism hidden by Southern sympathizers. Relighted June 28, 1866. it has not missed a night in over 100 years. Early keepers: Thomas Twiner, J. F. Papy, Wm. B. Davis, James A. Armour, Joseph A. Wells, Thomas Knight, Charles Seabrook. Operated by the United States Coast Guard since 1939.

ERECTED BY FLORIDA STATE SOCIETY. DAUGHTERS OF THE AMERICAN COLONISTS 1967

Jupiter Inlet Lighthouse. Photograph courtesy of Florida Division of Tourism.

Hillsboro Beach Lighthouse. Photograph courtesy of Florida Division of Tourism.

Florida Lighthouses

Hillsboro Beach Lighthouse

By the turn of the century, nearly all of the nation's hazardous shores had been marked, but the hurricane-lashed, eighty-mile stretch of coast between Jupiter Inlet and Key Biscayne was still dark. The logical site for a lighthouse to guard the northern approach to the burgeoning city of Miami was Hillsboro Inlet, named for the Earl of Hillsboro who was responsible for much of the surveying of Florida in the 1700s.

An iron-pile structure was deemed suitable for the relatively stable beach at Hillsboro. It would allow wind and water to pass through it unobstructed, but would not require the solid anchoring of screw-pile lighthouses. Six huge iron piles were sunk and a lantern was attached which was reached by a central stair cylinder. The lower third of the tower was painted white, and the upper two-thirds was made black to distinguish Hillsboro Beach Light from its red, masonry neighbors at Jupiter Inlet and Cape Florida.

The tower was completed in 1907 at a cost of $90,000 and it rose 136 feet. It was the last on-shore lighthouse built in Florida and is the state's most powerful beacon, visible nearly twenty-five miles at sea. A radiobeacon was added to the station following World War II. Its 75-foot antenna stands near the lighthouse.

The tower exhibits a white flash once every 20 seconds, but is partially obscured from the south. Its sturdy pile legs have stood firm through many hurricanes, including 1960's vicious Hurricane Donna which swirled tidal surge around its base. The light is a popular landmark with residents of nearby Deerfield Beach who fondly call its stretch of sand "Lighthouse Point."

Hillsboro Inlet Light Station in 1907. It now sits considerably closer to the high tide line due to erosion of the beach. Photograph courtesy of the National Archives.

Cape Florida Lighthouse. Photograph courtesy of Florida Division of Tourism.

8  *Florida Lighthouses*

Cape Florida Lighthouse

Courage, patience, and devotion are traits that have long been associated with lightkeepers. Their seige with wind, waves, fog and shipwreck was an undisputed occupational hazard, but for some the job required a dedication beyond the call of duty. At Cape Florida Lighthouse, on the southern tip of Key Biscayne, keepers tolerated heat, insects and savage hurricanes. In 1836, they endured an enemy even worse — the Seminoles.

The Cape Florida Lighthouse was among those first commissioned by Congress after Florida was annexed as a territory of the United States. Built in 1825, the sentinel saw an eventless first decade, but in March of 1835, during the Second Seminole War, an attack on the small population of what is today

Dade County left many dead, including the wife and children of Cape Florida lightkeeper William Cooley. The remaining survivors fled to Key West for safety. The bereaved Cooley was unable to carry on his duties as keeper, so the lighthouse was left in the care of his assistant keeper John Thompson and a black helper named Henry.

Only four months later, on a balmy afternoon in July, the Seminoles paddled out to Key Biscayne and attacked the lighthouse. Thompson and Henry took refuge in the tower. They managed to hold off the marauders until nightfall when a shower of bullets pierced the oil tanks and doused everything, including the men, with whale oil. The clever Seminoles then set fire to the lighthouse.

Thompson and his companion had no

Cape Florida Lighthouse, Key Biscayne, about the turn of the century. Photograph courtesy of the National Archives.

choice but to flee up to the lantern. The wooden stairway was quickly engulfed in flames. As the fire moved skyward, flames licked the iron floor of the lightroom. Its paint curled and burned away. Like fish trapped in a frying pan, the men clambered to the outer edges of the gallery, but were met with a shower of gunfire. Their dilemma was formidable — remain on the lantern and be burned alive, or step to the cooler rim to be shot.

In agony, Henry attempted to jump, but was shot and fell dead beside Thompson. Thinking to end his own suffering as well, Thompson crawled to a keg of gunpowder and rolled it into the inferno below him. The explosion rocked the tower from top to bottom, but instead of killing Thompson, it

caused the fire to drop to the base of the lighthouse and smolder. Naked and severely burned, Thompson lay dazed on the gallery. As the Seminoles retreated in their canoes, he lapsed into a painful sleep.

Thompson awoke the next morning to a grisly scene. Dead Indians were scattered all around the lighthouse compound, every flammable object was burned, and his sloop was gone. In addition, he was marooned on the 80-foot tower with no way to get down, and Henry's dead body had begun to reek in the summer heat. Regretfully, Thompson rolled his friend off the gallery. Mosquitoes tortured his raw flesh, and as noon approached and the heat of mid-July blazed down on him, the keeper passed out.

He awoke to voices and discovered a

schooner moored offshore. It was the USS *Motto*, a Navy ship. Her crew had heard Thompson's powder keg explode the day before and come to investigate. The *Motto*'s skipper could hardly believe his eyes when Thompson feebly called to be helped from the gutted tower-top. His clothes and hair had been burned off, and bullets had removed most of his fingers and toes. He looked more dead than alive, but the problem now was how to get him down.

Several ideas were tried, including a rope made airborne by a kite. Thompson remained patient, despite his pain, until a line fired from a musket providently snagged the lantern gallery. A tail block was hoisted for the keeper to secure. Two of the *Motto*'s crewmen then scaled the tower and lowered Thompson to safety on a makeshift litter. He was taken to a military hospital where he recovered, though somewhat crippled by his ordeal.

Indian trouble continued at Cape Florida and prevented the government from repairing and relighting the lighthouse until 1846. During reconstruction, it was discovered that the builder of the tower, Noah Humphreys of Massachusetts, had given it hollow walls, thereby ensuring fifty percent more profit. By 1855, Cape Florida Lighthouse was back in operation with solid walls, thirty feet of additional height, and the threat of Seminole attack gone.

In fact, the Indians had now become friendly with Cape Florida's lighthouse families.

One keeper's wife recalled going to awaken her children on a chilly morning to find a Seminole asleep with them. When questioned, the Indian claimed he had arrived in the night to barter, but wishing not to disturb the sleeping family, had crawled in bed to wait for daylight.

Cape Florida's lighthouse lens was severely damaged during the Civil War. It was repaired in 1867, but discontinued a decade later in favor of the beacon at nearby Fowey Rocks. Cape Florida Lighthouse remained dark a century, but in 1978 the Coast Guard decided to reinstate it. A hundred years after its decommissioning, a colorful ceremony placed it back in service on July 4, 1978.

Bill Baggs State Recreational Area was dedicated in 1966 in honor of the late newspaper editor who had urged its creation. The 406-acre tract encompasses an excellent beach and woodland retreat surrounding historic Cape Florida Lighthouse. The sentinel is listed on the National Register of Historic Places and is the oldest standing structure in South Florida.

Additional Information:

Bill Baggs Cape Florida State
  Recreational Area
1200 South Crandon Blvd.
Key Biscayne, FL 33149

9 *Florida Lighthouses*

The Reef Lighthouses

The Florida Keys are among several Atlantic locales which lay claim to the dismal reputation of "Graveyard of the Atlantic." Early charts referred to them as Islas de los Martires, or the Martyr Islands, suggesting the suffering of those whose vessels perished on the reefs. Millions of dollars in cargoes have been lost in the Florida Keys giving many of them the names of ill-fated vessels — Alligator, Fowey, Carysfort — and a string of giant iron lighthouses that are among the most unique exposed beacons in the world.

Sand Key, nine miles southeast of Key West, was given a traditional masonry tower in 1826, but its heavy walls rested on an unstable site and took a pummeling from South Florida's wind and waves. In an 1846 hurricane, it toppled, burying its lady keeper and

her five children in a watery grave. The disaster convinced the government that masonry towers were unsuitable for the Florida Reef, but lighthouse engineers would not give in to the sea-swept shoals.

A revolutionary lighthouse design consisting of iron piles screwed into the seabed had been successful in estuarine locations of England and the United States. The Lighthouse Service decided to adapt the design for South Florida's exposed reef. George Gordon Meade, who later led Union forces to victory at the Battle of Gettysburg, was assigned to oversee construction of the reef lights by the Army Corps of Engineers. As Sand Key's 80-foot brick lighthouse fell into the sea in 1846, the iron parts of Florida's first screwpile lighthouse, to be placed at Carysfort Reef,

Sand Key Lighthouse. Photograph courtesy of Florida Division of Tourism.

were being manufactured in a Philadelphia foundry.

Using a marine construction technique developed by English engineer Alexander Mitchell, George Gordon Meade anchored Carysfort Lighthouse's nine iron legs to the reef by means of huge flanged feet inserted through stabilizing discs. A keeper's house was built into the tower 33 feet above water, and a central stair cylinder led to the lantern 112 feet above sea. The structure's open framework design allowed wind and waves to pass through it unimpeded and exposed less surface area to the erosive elements of salt and spray.

Carysfort Reef Lighthouse was illuminated in March 1852, and a similar screwpile lighthouse was lit on Sand Key sixteen months later to replace its collapsed masonry tower. As Meade moved on to other lighthouse projects, a severe hurricane whirled over Sand

Carysfort Reef Lighthouse circa 1890. It replaced a lightship on the reef and was the first screwpile lighthouse built in the keys. Photograph courtesy of the National Archives.

The second Sand Key Lighthouse, built in 1853, replaced a masonry tower which collapsed in a storm in 1846. Photograph courtesy of the Library of Congress.

Key and washed it away. The lighthouse, however, remained firmly anchored to the reef beneath it as if it were part of it. Meade completed a third screwpile lighthouse at Sombrero Key and the beautiful brick sentinel at Jupiter Inlet before returning to active military duty during the Civil War.

By 1890, seven iron giants stood watch over the Florida Reef, from Fowey Rocks to Rebecca Shoal, and several more were added in the 1930s. They remain in service today with only slight modifications to modernize and automate their functions. Only Rebecca Shoal has required rebuilding. The others remain as firmly anchored into the Florida Reef as the day they were first illuminated.

Sombrero Lighthouse, at 142 feet, is the loftiest reef sentinel. Alligator Reef Lighthouse was the most expensive of these pile creations, costing $83,000 in 1873. The seventeen-mile range of Fowey Rocks Light makes

Fowey Rocks Lighthouse south of Miami with its tender anchored nearby for delivery of supplies. Circa 1890. Photograph courtesy of the National Archives.

it the keys' strongest beacon, but it is Carysfort Reef Lighthouse that conjures the most romance.

Carysfort's rusty red beacon was thought to harbor a poltergeist because of its nightly groaning and clanking sounds. Many keepers believed the ghost to be Captain Johnson who had kept the tower during its early years and died there tragically. The great-grandson of George Gordon Meade dispelled Carysfort's haunt when he discovered the tower's eerie noises arose from the rapid contraction of its metal braces as they cooled each night.

The Coast Guard has automated all of the reef lights, but in the days when keepers lived in the iron towers, duty was monotonous and, at times, frightening. During the 1938 hurricane, Carysfort Lighthouse rocked so badly one keeper became seasick. Hurricane Donna, in 1960, was even more harrowing for the reef keepers. With huge waves and near 200 mile-per-hour winds crashing through the towers, it was difficult to have faith in George Gordon Meade's designs, but the reef lights endured. During the 1980 Mariel Boat Lift, American Shoal Lighthouse was given attendant personnel whose job was to monitor the exodus of Cuban refugees and the flow of illegal contraband. Manning was only temporary, and the reef lights are again standing their night watches alone.

Alligator Reef Lighthouse. Photograph courtesy of U.S. Coast Guard.

Carysfort Reef Lighthouse. Photograph courtesy of U.S. Coast Guard.

The Reef Lights:

Fowey Rocks Lighthouse
Carysfort Reef Lighthouse
Sombrero Key Lighthouse
Alligator Reef Lighthouse
American Shoal Lighthouse
Sand Key Lighthouse
Pulaski Shoal Lighthouse

Rebecca Shoal Lighthouse
Cosgrove Shoal Lighthouse
Tennessee Reef Lighthouse
Smith Shoal Lighthouse
Pacific Reef Lighthouse
Molasses Reef Lighthouse

Additional Information:

Historic Key West Preservation Board
Key West, FL 33040

10 *Florida Lighthouses*

Key West Lighthouse

Through the years, Key West has known many reputations. Today it is one of Florida's most enticing vacation spots and lays claim to a piece of real estate pegged as the most southeastern point in the continental United States. Local "Conchs" boast of Key West's spectacular sunsets, gingerbread architecture, and relaxed island lifestyle, but they trace their heritage to a less honored group of South Florida citizens — the wreckers.

By fate, Key West lies in the midst of one of America's most dreaded sealanes. The dark blue Gulf Stream flows northeast just off the opaline waters of the Florida Reef, and ships sailing with it are given a comfortable five-knot push toward their destinations. West-bound shipping, however, must negotiate the perilous narrow strait between the Gulf Stream and the Reef. Littered about the sea-bed of South Florida lies proof that many vessels did not give the Reef a wide enough berth.

Situated at the center of this graveyard of ships, Key West became a haven for saints and sinners. A legitimate wrecking business took root in 1822 under the management of businessman John Watson Simonton, but free-booters and pirates clouded its operations. Stories of "mooncussing" surfaced, and some wreckers were accused of exhibiting false lights called "Judas Lanterns" to lure ships onto the reefs. There were even reports of outright piracy, but history reflects that the majority of Key West's wreckers were upright citizens who performed an invaluable service to the merchants and mariners whose cargoes foundered on the treacherous reefs.

The government was not blind to the navi-

Old Key West Lighthouse about 1880, situated on Whiteheads Point. Its height was later increased. Photograph courtesy of the National Archives.

gational hazards of South Florida, but bureaucratic holdups delayed progress in marking the keys until a few years after annexation. During these early territorial years, both Naval and civilian skippers complained of the keys' perils and pinpointed areas where lights were needed. As statistics were tabulated for Key West's first years as a salvage port, it became apparent that no stretch of American coastline swallowed more cargoes and crews.

Lighthouses were proposed for Key Biscayne, at the northeast fringe of the Reef, Key West at the center, and the Dry Tortugas on the west end. In addition, a lightship was to be anchored at Carysfort Reef, named for the unfortunate ship *Carysford* which fell prey to its razor-sharp grip in 1770.

Key West Lighthouse was built in 1825 on

Key West Lighthouse. Photograph courtesy of Florida Division of Tourism.

Whitehead Point. It was 85 feet tall, of brick construction, and held a fixed white light intensified by reflectors. It may have been an unpopular landmark with some of Key West's citizens who deemed its benevolent presence detrimental to the wrecking business, but in that same year $293,353 in wrecked cargo was auctioned off at Key West, proving that the lighthouse had not solved all the mysteries of the Reef.

Storms battered Whitehead Point yearly, and the lighthouse survived well until 1846. In October of that year, a monster corkscrew of wind and rain left Havana in ruins, then took Key West by surprise. Vessels in the harbor were tossed about like toys. Sand Key Lighthouse, nine miles offshore, disappeared in the churning surf with six persons aboard. Barbara Mabrity, keeper of Key West Lighthouse, barely escaped as the tower collapsed around her. Fourteen others, who had sought refuge in the lighthouse, drowned.

The government replaced Key West Lighthouse immediately with a 60-foot brick tower. About this time, officials approved plans to augment the chain of lights between Key Biscayne and the Dry Tortugas with screwpile lighthouses built directly on the Florida Reef. Added to the beams of shore lights, these aids would drastically reduce fatalities in South Florida. Key West Light-

house was further improved in the 1890s with the addition of 20 feet of height.

By 1969, Key West Lighthouse had outgrown its usefulness, primarily because creation of new real estate had left it far inland. The Coast Guard decided to discontinue it as a navigational aid. The Key West Art and Historical Society was operating a military museum adjacent to the lighthouse and asked to have the obsolete tower. Permission was granted, and the lighthouse plus many of its historic artifacts were added to the museum.

Key West Lighthouse is thought to be farther inland than any other American beacon. Visitors may climb its spiral stairs to judge for themselves how far from sea it has traveled since the heyday of the Key West wreckers. The tower stands in a balmy setting of palms and vines and its gallery offers one of the finest aerial views of the city and surrounding sea. The tower is one of the oldest structures in Key West and is located at 938 Whitehead Street.

Additional Information:

Key West Lighthouse and Military Museum
938 Whitehead Street
Key West, FL 33040

11 *Florida Lighthouses*

Dry Tortugas Lighthouses

Seventy miles west of Key West lies a cluster of seven islands famous for their seabirds, marine life, and an old fort that was once the citadel of the Gulf of Mexico. Ponce de Leon discovered these coral gems in 1513 and called them Las Tortugas, or The Turtles, because of the large number of turtles he found there. As centuries passed, mariners began calling these keys the Dry Tortugas because of their scorching heat and lack of fresh water.

Until 1821, when Florida became a territory of the United States, the Dry Tortugas were a popular pirate hangout. Vessels cruising the Florida Strait were easy prey, and the arid, sandy islets of the Dry Tortugas were excellent spots to hide treasure. Following annexation of Florida, the government drove out

the Dry Tortugas buccaneers and built a lighthouse on Garden Key to guide ships through this perilous section of the Gulf.

The first Garden Key lighthouse keeper, William Flaherty, might have had a more successful career were it not for his unhappy bride. Mrs. Flaherty, unlike most lightkeepers' wives, was unable to adjust to her lonely life on the remote Dry Tortugas. In a letter to First Lady Mrs. John Quincy Adams, she complained bitterly, pointing out the lack of social life at Garden Key, its heat, putrid cistern, relentless mosquitoes, and the infrequent delivery of fresh provisions. Shortly thereafter, William Flaherty was transferred to a mainland lighthouse.

In 1829, the Navy recommended a fortification be built on the Dry Tortugas to give the

Loggerhead Key Lighthouse at the Dry Tortugas replaced Garden Key Lighthouse in 1858.
Photograph courtesy of Florida Division of Tourism.

Fort Jefferson Lighthouse. Photograph courtesy of Florida Division of Tourism.

Dry Tortugas Lighthouse at Garden Key in the Gulf of Mexico. The keeper and his family are seen on the high porch. Circa 1890. Photograph courtesy of the National Archives.

United States a military advantage in the Gulf of Mexico. Construction of Fort Jefferson began in 1846 in a hexagonal shape incorporating the lighthouse into its south wall. The grandiose fort was to be one-half mile in circumference with 50-foot walls supporting three gun tiers and 450 guns. Slaves from the South performed most of the labor, but the awesome bastion was never completed, and its proposed garrison of 1500 men was never filled.

During the Civil War, Fort Jefferson saw no action, but Union deserters and Lincoln conspirators, including Dr. Samuel Mudd, who had unknowingly given medical aid to the President's assassin, were imprisoned there. Mudd was sentenced to life imprisonment at Fort Jefferson, but was released in 1869 because of his help during the devastating yellow fever epidemic at the fort in 1867.

As the war closed, engineers discovered that Fort Jefferson's walls had cracked due to a slow sinking of the structure. Tests showed that Garden Key was not a solid coral reef, as was formerly thought, but a build-up of sand and coral chunks. In addition to its instability, the fort had been rendered obsolete by the invention of the rifled cannon. The government had replaced Garden Key Lighthouse with a taller sentinel on nearby Loggerhead Key in 1858. As a result, Fort Jefferson was abandoned in 1874.

The Dry Tortugas became a wildlife refuge soon after the turn of the century to protect the endangered Sooty Tern. In 1935, Fort Jefferson was declared a National Monument and opened to the public. Today, its unique history and environment are preserved and interpreted by the National Park Service. It is a rare spot where one can enjoy a variety of activities from snorkeling and diving to roaming the remains of an old fort and lighthouse.

The Dry Tortugas are accessible by boat or amphibious aircraft from Key West. Visitors are cautioned to beware of the islands' harsh environment. They should bring their own supplies of food and water and prepare for prolonged periods of exposure to the sun and salt air.

Additional Information:

Superintendent
Everglades National Park/Fort Jefferson
   National Monument
Box 279
Homestead, FL 33030

12 *Florida Lighthouses*

Sanibel Island Lighthouse

Long before Sanibel Island was linked to the mainland by a causeway, Caloosa Indians paddled their canoes down the Caloosahatchee River to reach this jewel of a barrier island. Today Sanibel Island awaits the rush of shell-seekers only twenty miles south of busy Fort Myers. Because of its position facing northbound currents, Sanibel's beaches snare the Gulf's shells in abundance. Until its lighthouse was built on Ybel Point in 1884, it also snared an occasional misguided vessel.

The first settlers at Sanibel (spelled Senybal then) came from New York in 1833. These unfortunate pioneers were either massacred or driven out during the Indian Wars, but managed to ask the government for a lighthouse before their stay on the island ended. As commerce increased between Key West and Tampa, the subject of a lighthouse at Sanibel Island resurfaced, but it was 1883 before Congress could secure the land and finalize plans.

A pyramidal iron pile structure enclosing a 127-step spiral stair cylinder was designed for the wind-swept point. Parts for the lighthouse were manufactured in New Jersey and shipped to Florida, but the shipment was lost in the Gulf of Mexico only two miles from Point Ybel. Divers and salvors from Key West were called in, and all but two small brackets for the gallery were retrieved. These lost pieces were duplicated by a company in New Orleans and work began on the lighthouse. It was completed in August 1885 and illuminated with a third-order lens.

Henry Shanahan was Sanibel Lighthouse's

Sanibel Island Lighthouse. Photograph courtesy of Florida Division of Tourism.

first permanent keeper. His son served as his assistant. After several years at the lighthouse, Shanahan was left a widower with seven children. It was a lonely and difficult existence for him since the only other residents of the island, the Rutlands, lived several miles away. They had moved to Sanibel from Lake Apopka, but shortly after Mrs. Shanahan's death, Mr. Rutland also died.

Irene Rutland, widowed mother of five children, became the ideal candidate for the lightkeeper's second wife. Henry Shanahan proposed marriage. Since he was the only available man for miles around and held a respected government job, Irene Rutland happily consented. Together, the couple raised their twelve children, and later added a thirteenth child, as Sanibel Light's most memorable family.

In 1963, the solitude of Sanibel Island was broken by the opening of a causeway from the mainland. By then, the 104-foot Sanibel Lighthouse was under the care of the Coast Guard and had had its lens removed in favor of a modern electric beacon. Headquarters for the J. N. "Ding" Darling National Wildlife Refuge occupied its keeper's cottages. In November 1974, the old lighthouse and keepers' homes were placed on the National Register of Historic Places insuring their future preservation.

The Sanibel Island Lighthouse can be seen

from the causeway as you approach Sanibel
Island. It sits on Point Ybel at the terminus of
Lighthouse Road and has an excellent shelling beach popular for whelks, conchs, and
murex. Visitors may stroll the lighthouse
grounds, but the tower is closed to the public
due to its operative status.

Additional Information:

Sanibel/Captiva Islands Chamber
  of Commerce
Causeway Road
Sanibel, FL 33957

Old Port Boca Grande Lighthouse. Photograph by Sam Harris.

13 Florida Lighthouses

Gasparilla Island Lighthouses

In 1890, in order to illuminate the last dark spaces of the Florida coast, a lighthouse was lit on the southernmost tip of Gasparilla Island. Called Old Port Boca Grande Lighthouse, it served as a guidepost to Charlotte Harbor and was a square, house-type sentinel perched on steel stilts to protect it from the gnawing surf.

In 1927, the iron pile Gasparilla Island Rear Range Lighthouse was constructed north of the old lighthouse to serve as an additional aid for harbor-bound traffic. Like its sister sentinel at Sanibel Island, its open framework design allowed wind and water to pass through unobstructed, and its lightweight piles were more easily anchored in the Gulf Coast's erosive shore than a masonry foundation.

The stretch of coast over which these sen-tinels preside is a golden, shell-strewn strand flanked by whispering Australian pines and steeped in history and legend. Hardly a grain of sand in South Florida has not had some tale of piracy attached to it, and the sands of Gasparilla Island are no exception. Some residents of the island believe the body of a beautiful Spanish princess lies buried near the old lighthouse and that her headless ap-parition occasionally appears on the beach.

Gasparilla Island received its name from the buccaneer José Gaspar who was thought to have used it as a haven for his leisure hours. Gaspar was a man of intense greed and violence, prone to outbursts of temper and extravagant displays of behavior. His two loves in life were riches and beautiful women, and he set about obtaining them with cutthroat passion. His many kidnapped female victims were sequestered on a small island only a few miles south of Boca Grande. He called it *Cautiva,* which means female prisoner, but we know it today as Captiva Island.

At some point in Gaspar's voyages, he captured a vessel with a beautiful Spanish princess on board. Her name was Josefa, and Gaspar fell helplessly in love with her. As he sailed to Gasparilla Island with his enchanting prize, he begged her repeatedly to marry him, but she refused. In a final act of defiance, the princess cursed Gaspar and spat in his face. Though he had shown uncharacteristic restraint in his pursuit of the girl, her insult was more than he could bear. He brandished his saber and, in a fit of rage, beheaded her.

Gaspar wept bitterly over the impulsive act and tenderly carried the princess' body ashore at Gasparilla Island. There he buried her in the sand, but wishing to keep some treasure of the unconsummated love affair, Gaspar took the girl's head back to his ship and put it in a jar. Thereafter, sailors reported seeing a headless figure combing the beach at Gasparilla Island in search of its missing head. Perhaps the bright beams of Gasparilla's lighthouses have soothed the unsettled spirit, for she is reported less and less as years go by.

Old Port Boca Grande Lighthouse was abandoned in 1967 and fell victim to vandals and the elements. Gasparilla Island Rear Range Lighthouse continues in operation as an automatic beacon, but with an uncertain future, since the beach surrounding it is constantly eroding.

Local residents felt the elder sentinel should be preserved and had it transferred from federal to county ownership on February 11, 1972 for inclusion in a park. It was placed on the National Register of Historic Places in 1980. Late in 1985, the Gasparilla

Island Conservation and Improvement Association assumed the responsibility of restoring the rapidly deteriorating structure. The project — financed in part with historic preservation grant assistance provided by the Bureau of Historic Preservation, Florida Department of State, assisted by the Historic Preservation Advisory Council — was successfully completed in November 1986. Through the assistance of the U.S. Coast Guard, the original imported French Fresnel lens was reinstalled. On November 21 of that year the beacon was ceremoniously relit and the Old Boca Grande Lighthouse is again an active federal aid to navigation.

Currently, work continues on the interior of the old lighthouse which will serve as both an office for the Department of Natural Resources' resident ranger and a local maritime museum.

Both of Gasparilla Island's lighthouses can be reached via a toll bridge and causeway from Placida on Route 771. Gasparilla Island Rear Range Lighthouse sits about halfway down the island, and the Old Port Boca Grande Lighthouse watches over the island's southernmost point.

Evening is perhaps the ideal time to visit the lighthouses and their beautiful, tawny beaches. As the sun falls behind the old tower, it appears in the lantern for a moment, illuminating the intricate French lens like a huge, orange beacon, then disappears into the Gulf just as the sentinel's flashing white light comes to life.

Additional Information:

Gasparilla Island Conservation &
    Improvement Association
P.O. Box 446
Boca Grande, FL 33921
(813) 964-2667

Gasparilla Rear Range Lighthouse. Photograph by Jonathan De Wire.

Gasparilla Rear Range Lighthouse. Photograph by Jonathan De Wire.

14 *Florida Lighthouses*

Egmont Key Lighthouse

The sea road to Tampa Bay has been guarded by Egmont Key Lighthouse since 1848, though its importance as a port predates the beacon by many years. Spanish explorer Hernando de Soto began his voyage to the Mississippi River from Tampa in 1539, and the United States Army established the first settlement at Tampa in 1823 with the building of Fort Brooke. When Tampa's importance as the gateway to South and Central America was recognized, the government built a small lighthouse on the low sandy key at the entrance to the bay.

Constructed at a cost of $7,050, it was illuminated for the first time in 1848. Later that year, a hurricane struck the Gulf coast and destroyed the lighthouse. The lightkeeper and his family barely managed to escape and rode

out the storm lying in the bottom of the station boat, which the keeper had tethered to a palm tree.

Egmont Key remained dark for a decade, until a new, 85-foot lighthouse was built on the northern end of the key. It was painted white to showcase it against Tampa Bay's turquoise water. Just two years later the Civil War broke out, and Confederate forces put out the light and damaged the lantern.

The Union Army later regained the island and used it as a staging point for the Tampa Bay blockade. Toward the end of the war, Confederate prisoners were kept on Egmont Key, along with protected runaway slaves and Union sympathizers. The lighthouse, however, was not relit until 1866.

During the Spanish-American War, the

Egmont Key Lighthouse at St. Petersburg has lost its classical lantern and lens to a modern aeromarine beacon. Photograph courtesy of Florida Division of Tourism.

Egmont Key Lighthouse. Photograph courtesy of Florida Division of Tourism.

United States built more fortifications on Egmont Key to counteract a possible Spanish invasion, but no shots were ever fired. After the Spanish were defeated in Cuba, the three hundred men assigned to Egmont Key were transferred and the lighthouse keeper was once again alone on the island.

Egmont Key Lighthouse is still in service with a white beacon flashing once every fifteen seconds and visible twenty-two miles at sea. Though the lighthouse runs automatically, its radiobeacon, emitted from a 133-foot antenna, is operated by resident Coast Guard personnel.

A foghorn also operates at the station during periods of poor visibility. Though fog is uncommon in Florida waters, Tampa Bay is occasionally plagued by mists. Egmont Key's groaning horn blasts twice a minute, shattering the silence with urgent warnings for vessels traveling beneath the Sunshine Skyway Bridge. With more than 20,000,000 tons of cargo coming in and out of Tampa Bay each year, little Egmont Key Lighthouse and its fog signal perform a critical service.

Egmont Key is accessible only by boat, but the lighthouse is visible from Fort de Soto Park.

15  Florida Lighthouses

St. Marks Lighthouse

St. Marks was settled by the Spaniards in the 1700s, and evidence indicates they may have had a marker of sorts at the mouth of the St. Marks River to guide ships. It was not until 1828 that a lighthouse was built at Florida's "Big Bend." It was so poorly constructed the local collector of customs rejected it and ordered a second tower built. This sturdier sentinel, erected by Calvin Knowlton, was 73 feet tall, with solid brick walls, and went into service in 1831. It was only a few years old when erosion threatened to undermine it. The government opted to move it rather than build a new tower. Mr. Knowlton was given the contract to relocate it nearby.

St. Marks Lighthouse's keeper requested protection during the Seminole War, but was inexplicably denied both a guard and a boat for escape. Fortunately, the Indians ignored the beacon, and, unlike Cape Florida Lighthouse, St. Marks Light was unharmed.

During the Civil War, Confederates attempted to blow up the lighthouse, but only succeeded in damaging an eight-foot section of its lower walls. It was repaired immediately following the war and returned to service January 8, 1867. A decade later, it was repointed and partially rebuilt.

In 1931, St. Marks National Wildlife Refuge was established, encompassing 31,500 acres of water and 65,000 acres of land, including the St. Marks Lighthouse. The refuge is one of the oldest in the National Wildlife Refuge System and protects such natural populations as alligators, Canada geese, and Southern bald eagles.

In addition, preservation has been provided

St. Marks Lighthouse. Photograph courtesy of Florida Division of Tourism.

St. Marks Lighthouse. Photograph courtesy of Florida Division of Tourism.

for the St. Marks Lighthouse. It is a dedicated site listed in the National Register of Historic Places. The tower itself is maintained as an active aid by the Coast Guard and is visible twenty miles at sea. It is accessible for exterior viewing at the terminus of S-59. Picnic facilities, hiking trails and a boat launch are also available near the lighthouse.

Additional Information:

Refuge Manager
St. Marks National Wildlife Refuge
Box 68
St. Marks, FL 32355

16 *Florida Lighthouses*

Cape St. George Lighthouse

Apalachicola Bay is shielded from the Gulf of Mexico by a thin, forty-mile strip of bleached sand known as St. George Island. The southernmost point of this strand juts out into the Gulf at Cape St. George before curving north toward St. Vincent Island. Firmly anchored in its sands is Cape St. George Lighthouse, a hurricane-battered beacon that has guarded the bay for a century and a half.

Cape St. George gained a dreadful reputation early in its history when the ship *Tiger* struck a ledge off the cape in 1766. The crew and passengers managed to get ashore, but soon discovered they were marooned on an island. They subsisted on bivalves until a week later when local Indians arrived to hunt and fish at the cape.

The Indians seemed friendly at first and of- fered to take the castaways to the mainland. A few days later, however, they abandoned them on a tiny isle. The starving group dwindled until only a woman and two men remained. The trio put together a crude raft and finally reached the mainland in mid-April. Crazed with hunger, the woman and one man attacked their companion and resorted to cannibalism to survive.

As they walked east, a forest fire providently left burned animals in its wake for food. Insects so tormented the pair they used the hide of a dead alligator to cover their faces and feet. The first week of May they were finally rescued by British soldiers. It had been eighty-one days since the *Tiger* wrecked at Cape St. George.

The formidable fate of this ship was long

85

Cape St. George Lighthouse. Photograph courtesy of Florida Division of Tourism.

forgotten when Cape St. George Lighthouse blinked on in 1833. The $11,400 tower rose 65 feet and held thirteen lamps intensified by reflectors. Fourteen years later, a new lighthouse was built two miles from the original one. It lasted only four years before being toppled in a storm.

A third lighthouse was built in 1852, and, though damaged in the Civil War and washed by many fierce storms, it survives today. Confederates destroyed the keeper's quarters and damaged the delicate lens. It was restored to the lantern at the end of the war, but engineers later discovered a dark spot in its field and had to replace it with a new lens.

During World War II, the lighthouse served as a "Coastal Lookout Station" for the Gulf of Mexico. Today, its white, conical form is a popular landmark with Cape St. George visitors. The island, part of Cape St. George State Reserve, is accessible only by private boat. The lighthouse sits about five miles from the dock and is reached by foot. This is a trek for the hearty, but well worth the effort.

Additional Information:

Apalachicola Bay Chamber of Commerce
45 Market Street
Apalachicola, FL 32320

17  *Florida Lighthouses*

Cape San Blas Lighthouse

No lighthouse station in the South has endured worse torment than Cape San Blas Lighthouse between Apalachicola and Port St. Joe. In 1838, Congress appropriated $10,000 for a lighthouse on the northern tip of Cape San Blas. Dubbed St. Joseph Bay Lighthouse, its career lasted only a decade before Congress decided to build a second lighthouse further south on the cape.

This new tower stood 85 feet tall and was operative only three years when a storm collapsed it. The old St. Joseph Bay Lighthouse also toppled. A successor was lit in 1856, but washed away in a hurricane the following summer. Undaunted, Congress authorized a fourth tower, which was lit in 1858. This time it was not nature which destroyed the lighthouse, but Confederates. The tower's third-

order lens was damaged and the entire station burned. In 1865, the government again rebuilt.

This fifth sentinel was 96 feet above sea level and sported a revolving light visible sixteen miles. A red sector in the beacon warned of treacherous shoals extending five miles out from the cape's elbow. In 1870, the sea began to nudge the tower base during heavy storms. Erosion continued in a devastating yearly cycle until the lighthouse toppled in 1882.

A 90-foot-tall log with a light on top of it served as a beacon until the sixth Cape San Blas Lighthouse was completed in 1885. This time the government opted for a skeleton tower with a central stair cylinder surrounded by iron pile legs, but construction was ham-

This old photo, circa 1881, is believed to be the third tower built at Cape San Blas. Photograph courtesy of the Florida State Archives.

pered by drought, mosquitoes, and the near loss of building materials when their vessel sank. Salvage was accomplished and the 90-foot tower was completed in 1885 at a safe distance 900 feet inland.

Engineers felt sure erosion would no longer plague the station, but by 1889, the distance between the tower and the sea had shortened to 200 feet. As the government assessed the possibility of moving the lighthouse, an 1894 storm swallowed the remainder of the beach, toppled the keeper's house, and left the lighthouse standing in water. Congress debated over a safe location for the Cape San Blas Lighthouse. Meanwhile, the cycle of erosion reversed, and sand began to build up along the point.

The tower was stabilized until 1916 when the action of the sea again reversed and erosion threatened. The lighthouse was finally moved in 1918 to a safe location 1,857 feet north. It remains there today and incorporates a Loran Station. The toppled St. Joseph Bay Lighthouse was replaced in 1902 by the "Beacon Hill Lighthouse" on the mainland near Port St. Joe, but was discontinued in favor of a 78-foot skeleton tower in 1960.

Additional Information:

Apalachicola Bay Chamber of Commerce
45 Market Street
Apalachicola, FL 32320

Pensacola Lighthouse. Photograph by Jonathan De Wire.

18  *Florida Lighthouses*

Pensacola Lighthouse

The designation of Pensacola as the site of a Navy yard spurred the government to build a lighthouse there. It was lit in 1825 at the southern entrance to Pensacola Bay on a 40-foot bluff and was the first United States lighthouse built on the Florida Gulf Coast. Its revolving light fell short of providing assistance to ships using Pensacola's deep, natural harbor. Trees on both the mainland and nearby Santa Rosa Island obscured its beam, and the light of its ten lamps was extremely inadequate. After many complaints, including one that pointed out its similarity to nearby Mobile Light, the lighthouse was replaced with a 171-foot tower on the north side of the bay entrance.

This new beacon was given a first-order lens with a range of twenty-one miles. Its durability was tested in the Civil War by repeated gunfire, but no noticeable damage was done. Confederates did manage to dismantle and remove the lens. It was hidden and a temporary beacon served in its place until it was located in 1869.

Lightning struck Pensacola Lighthouse in 1875 and melted some of its metal interior. Three years later, cracks appeared in the tower walls, attributed to the combined elements of storms, lightning, and shelling during the war. The lighthouse was repointed and given its present daymark of black and white. It suffered no more difficulties other than a rare Gulf Coast earthquake in 1885 that momentarily stopped the station clock and rocked the expensive Fresnel lens.

The Pensacola Lighthouse is today located

Pensacola Lighthouse.
Photograph courtesy of Florida Division of Tourism.

on Pensacola Naval Air Station. It remains active, though automated, and its keeper's quarters have been converted into the "Lighthouse Apartments" which may be rented on a daily basis. Permission to visit the lighthouse for exterior viewing can be secured at the main gate of Pensacola Naval Air Station.

Additional Information:

"Lighthouse Apartments"
Oak Grove Park
Naval Air Station
Pensacola, FL 32508

Lighthouse Societies and Clubs

U.S. Lighthouse Society
244 Kearny St., 5th Floor
San Francisco, CA 94108
(415) 362-7255

Pharos Lighthouse Study Unit
19735 Scenic Harbor Drive
Northville, MI 48167

Great Lakes Lighthouse Keepers Association
P.O. Box 80
Allen Park, MI 48101

Suggested Reading

General History:

Adamson, H.C. *Keepers of the Lights.* NY: Greenburg Press, 1955.

Beaver, Patrick. *A History of Lighthouses.* Secaucus, NJ: Citadel Press, 1973.

Holland, Francis Ross Jr. *America's Lighthouses.* Brattleboro, VT: Stephen Greene Press, 1972.

Snow, Edward Rowe. *Famous Lighthouses of America.* NY: Dodd Mead Co., 1955.

Regional History:

(West Coast)

Gibbs, James. *Lighthouses of the Pacific.* West Chester, PA: Shiffer Publishing Co., 1986.

(Great Lakes)

Hyde, Charles. *The Northern Lights.* Lansing, MI: Michigan Dept. of Natural Resources, 1986.

(New England)

Snow, Edward Rowe. *The Lighthouses of New England.* NY: Dodd Mead Co., 1973.

(Mid-Atlantic)

DeGast, Robert. *The Lighthouses of the Chesapeake Bay.* Baltimore, MD: Johns Hopkins University Press, 1973.

Stick, David. *North Carolina Lighthouses.* Raleigh, NC: Dept. of Cultural Resources, 1980.

(Southeast)

Cipra, David. *Lighthouses of the Northern Gulf of Mexico.* Washington, D.C.: GPO, 1976.

Kagerer, Rudy. *Guidebook To Lighthouses in South Carolina, Georgia, and Florida East Coast.* Athens, GA: Lighthouse Publications, 1985.

Index